Belinda Blinked;
Belinda Blumenthal's Business Tips for
Go Getters;

A Life Tips book from Belinda
Blumenthal & Rocky Flintstone.

Author;

Rocky Flintstone;

Belinda Blumenthal;

Belinda Blumenthal.
Is a successful international Sales Director in her own right. In this book she outlines the secrets of her success and how you can emulate her. Ms. Blumenthal uses many examples from her own workplace to emphasise how you too can become a top go getter.

Rocky Flintstone.
Is a writer of some repute. Having written a best selling mini series entitled 'Belinda Blinked' he has teamed up with Belinda Blumenthal to produce a book which details the business tips he and Ms. Blumenthal have successfully used in their business careers to date.

Contents;

Conclusion;

By Sir James Godwin;
Chairman, Steele's Pots and Pans;

Flintstone approached me a year or so ago asking if I'd write a little something for the start of a business pamphlet he was working on with an ex-employee of mine, Ms. Blumenthal. Naturally it would have been churlish of me to refuse, even though my parting with Ms. Blumenthal was not on very good terms, and here we are. Now in writing such a missive I decided to take good advice and as such invited the remnants of the Glee Team to the Pentra for afternoon tea and a brainstorming session. Needless to say, it was a complete waste of time. No one brought a flip chart and Giselle insisted on playing with her brassiere. Bella sent

Donna in her place who didn't contribute a dam thing. I say remnants, because Blumenthal has been fired and Maeve is in a US top security prison. Hrrmmph, need I say more?

Needless to say, once the tea and cream buns were eaten and the Gin and Tonics started to flow things improved... for instance, Bella turned up and sent the ineffective Donna back to the office to find her missing love bullets.

I then asked the girls their thoughts on how a business such as Steele's should be run. The overall point that was quite forcibly made to me was one of friendship and professionalism. Personally, I like to think this is the essence of Steele's with the Glee Team being a prime example. Now I am the first to admit that at times their techniques can be quite risqué but I always know that the job will get done... somehow.

Professionalism is a word bandied around quite a lot these days and I have to note Mr Flintstone and Ms Blumenthal ignore it completely... mind you to be completely honest I've only read the chapter headings... however my good pal, Clarence the Duke of Epsom, got stuck into the chapter on Self Belief... and then we had to go to his club. Hrrmmph, never mind how that ended, let's just say he ran out of lipstick...

The disappointing thing to me about Mr Flintstone and Ms Blumenthal's book is its lack of long words... all academic books on business practice should be littered with these gems. But no, they are sadly missing. The Glee Team didn't agree with me of course, but as I'm the Chairman, I had my way... this time.

That of course brings me to my last point, for true job satisfaction you have to become the CEO... every other bugger must obey you and power is the ultimate accolade. Being Chairman doesn't cut the mustard and that is something I too have to come to grips with... my own personal crusade so to speak.

I sadly notice Flintstone and Blumenthal don't mention this either...

Introduction;

Whilst the principals of this book can equally be used by men, it has been mostly aimed at women for three simple reasons.

1. I, Belinda Blumenthal am a woman working in a tough business environment.

2. Most books of this kind are written for men by men. Rocky doesn't really count as he's a co-author, even if he thinks he's the author.

3. Women often want different things to men from their business success.

When you start out in the business world it's essential to work out what you want to achieve. As Tony my old M.D keeps saying, "if you don't have a destination, it will be hard to find your way there!" Thanks Tony!

Are you happy to start at the bottom and work your way up the same organisation just like Giselle, or do you want to move jobs regularly, each time for more money and responsibility. As you already know I'm continually having to adapt as I've moved companies many times. I also have to be in control of my subordinates and having had four RSM's and a couple of Key Account Managers reporting to me at Steeles Pots and Pans was demanding to say the least. My new role as Chief Exec of the Herstellung is even more exacting and the addition of deciding who I can trust makes it even harder.

I've also learnt along the way that some people like Sir James Godwin are impossible to please but you should never stop trying. Once you do, it's time to get out, or you'll be pushed out... as he pushed me out. I think looking back at that time of my career, that injustice was the hardest thing I've ever had to endure. Hence my picking up some espionage work for the Duchess.

Passion is what drives a top business woman on and if you can't feel passionate about your job then find one you do! I keep saying this to Giselle, because she feels she's under employed being a sales account manager. Bella however started to flourish and I needed to watch her...

very carefully. As you now know, I didn't lookout for myself terribly well and that was my mistake.

I didn't particularly enjoy the pots and pans business and as you know I found the name Steele's Pots and Pans abhorrent. I do however enjoy business itself, the buzz of getting the sale, meeting the customers, developing my staff and seeing the company grow. I think Des Martin was one of my better successes... from a snivelling, about to resign Regional Sales Manager, to a successful Managing Director is an amazing job development path. So, add job satisfaction to your list of essential elements for a top career and go for it!

Chapter 1

What you need to succeed;

A Brain;
God help Bella... no I'm joking!
It's helpful to think hard (not that sort
of hard) about things before you do
them and thought before action should
be your mantra. However, don't
analyse so much that you get 'analysis
paralysis' which will mean you never do
anything. When Tony put me in that
Maze, I was lucky in that he hadn't
prepped me fully on what was going to
happen. If he had I might have fluffed
the whole episode, as it was, it was a
fantastic success.

A "Can Do" Attitude;

Fear of failure is very real and so is the fear of what other people may say. This is why it helps to have mentors; if you can't find a real person like me then use books and digital stuff to help you keep going. I'm lucky in that I have Cristina and Peter Rouse to bounce ideas off. Jim Stirling is also very supportive and he's a real out of the box thinker which can be very stimulating. Remember if you put your head above the parapet you must expect to get shot at! Every time Tony summons me to his office I go prepared to be shouted at, the fact it hasn't happened yet is just luck! As for Sir James Godwin... all he knows is how to shout and make money.

Personal Character;

This is very important and it really helps if you can relate to being an extrovert. Business is all about people and if you want to succeed in business you need to communicate. That means getting to know people better... like the Schweinsteigers or Penelope Pollet. Don't overlook people like Jim Thompson who might work for you or even somewhere else in the organisation. If they have an input to your success, they're a valuable ally. To be honest, I never really got on with Iain Snail or Bill in HR, so that was my failure, not theirs.

Basic Maths;
Being numerate (ability to understand numbers) is important as is the ability to know exactly where things stand at any time. Maeve was brilliant at this sort of thing, but saying that, she

turned out to be so twisted it was all a fearful waste of her talent. This is an area many women need to work on and if you are one of them knowing your weaknesses means you are dealing with it.

Always keep control of what money you're spending, your costs in technical jargon, this is called 'good defence.' That's what I was doing when I made Jim Thompson put the cost of the pickup from Heathrow airport on the two regional sales managers cost centres. If I hadn't done this, that cost would have gone against my department as a whole, why should I give those two guys a free ride?

Be Adaptable;
You'll have to accept that you'll always be learning and constantly changing to keep your job and to develop through

the company. That's why I strongly believe in relevant training courses. You'll also become a better person through the process of working for the company and you'll learn to know yourself better. This was one of the major benefits of our sales training exercise in Cornwall. By its end we all knew what we needed to concentrate our learning skills on, it was a pity that Bella's turned out to be how to drive a car.

Give Value and good Service;
This is something women tend to be good at, everyone wants quality and value especially the Peter Rouse and Jim Stirling's of this world. Try to go that extra mile, it will really pay off. In that maze I could have just brushed off Jim Stirling as a no hoper, I didn't, I

went that extra inch and boy did that pay off!

Your USP;
Try to isolate your Unique Selling Point. You could say my USP is my glamourous hair and very attractive body, it doesn't matter what it is, just know what yours is. You might be able to calm down irate customers, or deliver the best presentations ever. Your USP should be what you are the best at in your organisation.

Control your Reactions;
You can't always control what happens to you, but you can control your reaction to it. You may have had a bad day but events will not be made better by you falling to pieces.

Keep thinking and trying to find a way out and you will, stand back and reassess the situation. When the Duchess put me in that horse box, I didn't have many options, so I waited and had a few of the gin and tonics that were left lying around, they helped to relax me and of course everything turned out just great. She's still a shit driver and I wonder if I should send her and Bella on an advanced learning to drive course?

Be a good Manager;
As women we do seem to have a knack of understanding people and good staff are very important to every organisation. That's why we don't want to lose them to a fit of temper or frustration over their individual needs. Des Martin for example could easily have resigned that afternoon in the

office, but with a bit of coaxing I found out what was really bothering him. He didn't really want to resign he just needed a bit of tender care. I'm good at that and Des went back into his empty life a renewed man full of vigour and hope for the future. That's called good management. Bella was the same, she started off as a receptionist and now she's an International Sales Director... and unfortunately from my current position, making a really good job of it!

Multi-Tasking;
We women are way better at this than men and this is an essential skill in any company. Giselle is one of the best people I know at this sort of thing. That's why Tony was so reluctant to promote her, he was useless, but with Giselle helping him out, it was made easy for him. Oh, don't tell him I said

that of course as he's now CEO! Of course, what we all didn't know at the time, was that Giselle was also multi-tasking for Herr Bisch as the "Special One". I rest my case.

Be a good Communicator;
Women are less confrontational than men. We don't seem to have as much a problem with our egos, that means we can take our time and get our point across. Good communication is vital in today's fast paced business world. When I first met the youngish man, I had to work quite hard at getting him to understand my needs, but he came through, even though the restaurant took last orders at that stupid time of the evening. Later that night when he turned up with the ice, turkey sandwiches and bottle of Chardonnay you could say it was a win-win for us

both. Good communication means a win-win for both parties. Some people like Sir James might call it a compromise, but if done right you'll have the best solution and the opportunity to do even more business. When he fired me, he should have taken a beat and put me on holiday leave... it was only a week at most that I was out of action, but he pulled the trigger and of course the rest is history. He failed to communicate and as such we are where we are. Thank you, Sir James.

Be Observant;
Always be aware of your surroundings and what is going on around you. Be observant and look for body language clues from the person you are engaging with. I could write a book on body language alone it's such a big topic and

to be honest Natasha Biles our training guru has already done so... well its half written and she's waiting on me and Rocky to finish our respective bits.

In a nutshell people give away their true feelings through their body posture and actions. These are always non-spoken. I'll always remember when I took the RSM's to the Bull and Rushes pub during our first regional Sales meeting. You remember, I had to do that water on the nipples technique to get my message across to them. That was pure body language and they eventually got it. I was essentially saying, hey guys, I may be female with female bits... very nice female bits I might add, but we're all a member of one team. My Glee Team drove the message home when we finished up at the Pentra, all those RSM's left wanting more without any words being spoken... and our sales increased!!

Be Well Presented;
We women are used to being judged on our appearance. It's a fact of life and I love it. Use it to your advantage without being too over the top. Men have a tougher time as to be overdressed for them can make them look like a dandy. Peter Rouse comes to mind, but then he's Dutch, Helga of course could try much harder... but of course she's really an FBI agent under cover.
I think the Duchess has it right, smart looking and professional with a bit of sexual appeal thrown in... have you seen her in riding clothes?

Be Inquisitive;

Always ask questions about what is going on around you. Men hate to do this and it is a weakness you can build on. The only stupid question is the one you don't ask. Never do something you don't understand, it's a quick road to disaster. My RSM's always said I ask too many questions when I'm with their customers, but by understanding the situation you're in, you can make a better decision. Jim Thompson is the exception to the rule, he won't leave my office until he's 100% sure of what he has to do, that's why he never makes big mistakes... I mean Peggy Strumpethouse was a BIG mistake, but again that was in his personal life.

Be Diligent;
Even as a student in the sixth form it was obvious that girls always work harder and do their homework when

compared to the boys. That's a strength we can use in later life. We're also better organised and combining diligence with organisation and communication means you'll be a winner. That's why Giselle could eventually become the MD of Steele's Pots and Pans, that and her extreme ambition... of course that depends on if Sir James ever forgives her for the Bisch double cross.

Be a Networker;
This is something a lesser mortal would call gossiping. Take time to network at work, we women do it naturally and we don't need the golf course like our male compatriots. My old original Glee Team of Giselle, Bella and myself had all the ingredients needed to find out anything that went on in Steeles. I had the word from the customers, Bella controlled

the front door and Giselle saw all the privileged information that came across Tony's desk... awesome!

Networking makes sense and it can also be a very social thing to do... especially on a Friday afternoon at the Pentra.

Don't be too Risk Averse;
Women can often be seen by men as being risk adverse. This of course works both ways and it can mean we won't take a risk which could be bad for the organisation. However, if we do take that risk then you can be sure we'll have thought it through and protected the downside if anything goes wrong. This is very important as to survive in corporate life you'll have to learn to deal with things going wrong.
Remember taking risks is a necessary part of life. I wouldn't have made the inroads into Peter Rouse's organisation

if I hadn't taken a, perhaps silly, risk of blowing a kiss at Cristina's ass when I first met her. That one small action paid off big time and I now see them both socially at least every four weeks. Amsterdammm is so rewarding as a major city! Besides, I also get to spend some time with Helga… networking!

So, there you have it, always remember that success breeds success. We women have everything we need to make it in the business world and don't ever forget it! If you need more proof, then just look at Bella!

It sounds obvious but this is essential and even people who sometimes get a lucky break have to work hard. Bella has always been a hard worker and her promotion came about because of this and of course her very special relationship with Jim Stirling. I always had to work hard, even at school and college. I seldom watched TV which can be a big distraction and once you get used to working it's not so bad and is much easier when you are young than when you are older. To be honest, I just don't know how the Duchess does it... I guess she just delegates to minions such as my old lover James Sp00ner, may he rest in peace.

In business the buck stops with you and if you don't take responsibility and do it no one else will. If they do you may find yourself out of a job. One of the original gripes I had from the RSM's was that they were never given the responsibility to do their job. Everything was done with a bottle of Scotch from head office. I changed that situation pretty quickly by empowering them and it didn't take long for their sales to increase.

Women are good at taking responsibility as many of you have to run a home, children and a job, hard work is what we're used to.

Hard work will mean you'll eventually get more things done and become more productive. That is what will become noticed by your superiors, so focus on the tasks and keep track of what you do. Bite sized goals are important if you start to feel overwhelmed by the size of your workload. Set up a chart and begin to plot the figures, As I said earlier, Jim Thompson really gets motivated when we do our weekly update. We can see the progress we're achieving... and yes, sometimes it's not all positive, but at least we know we have to change something and that's all part of the hard work we put into the job.

Be disciplined at all times and the hard work will get easier. Remember the road to hell is paved with good intentions, you must continually remember this job is not going to do itself. When you set your goals, remember to set a deadline, even if it's only for your own benefit. Then focus to deliver the project. I like to think about past diets and what I had to do to succeed, it may sound corny, but use the same techniques! Cristina Rouse and I always have this conversation each time we get together, we try to eat better and more sensibly, though we do lapse a little bit with the Chardonnay. But hey, a girl does have to relax!

Cristina herself is very disciplined and is always setting goals, I think it's one of her assets Peter really likes! He of course likes a lot of my assets as well...

Always think before you take action, having the time to assess a problem or situation is very important. One of my mentors called
Stephen Covey an American lifestyle and business Guru calls this a pause button. Hank Skank did exactly this when he took me to see the Krankies play in Dallas. He wasn't as sold on us

as Jim was and he decided to press the pause button and check us out, I'm glad he did, because the whole project has blossomed way beyond our initial hopes.

I always think back to Sir James and my last fateful discussion with him when he fired me... if he'd just hit his pause button, everything would have been so very different.

Hard work and thinking of course, is hard, as another American, Mr Ford of the Ford Motor Company said, 'it's why so few people do think.'

Hard work also goes hand in hand with perseverance. It's easy to get discouraged as Des Martin did when he and his wife split up. Some people will make you feel terrible even though they don't mean to, Sir James has a knack for this. If you are to succeed you must keep on working, start and keep going. Of course, this is a lot easier than it sounds especially when no one else around you is doing it. This is why mentors are needed and I'm lucky to have the Rouse's whom I can actually talk to. Most likely your mentors will be in the form of books or digital stuff as it's hard, though not completely impossible, to find real people. Talking to Rocky, is always a good shout for me.

Chapter 3

Technology and the Internet;

The world is changing fast and you need to move with it, it's important to embrace change, new trends are your friend. Be an early adopter, which means try new things and learn new skills the most important of which is I.T.…. information technology. I do feel that Steele's Pots and Pans are a little behind the curve ball when it comes to technology. I mean that fax machine in Jim Thompson's office should have been binned years ago. But you know, waste not, want not and sometimes… just sometimes, it turns out to be really useful!

The internet has changed the world forever, you can look at it as the new frontier. Younger people like us have a tremendous advantage over older people, we can seize change whilst they may be wary of it. The internet is not just about websites but also social media such as Twitter... sorry X, Facebook and blogs. In fact, these areas are now so important a lot of companies are hiring specialists. At Steele's they hadn't done that whilst I was there... Iain Snail is on it I believe, but he's so slow at getting things done for obvious reasons... (his name???) But lots of companies do farm this sort of thing out to independent professionals and good for them.

Technology is extremely important and you should ensure you are keeping up with it. This not only means using word processing software, but also spreadsheets etc... never mind the ever invasive AI... Artificial Intelligence.

Don't get left behind!

Chapter 4

There are two important areas where planning is essential for anyone in business. The first is your game plan for your personal advancement up through the organization. The second is your planning for your actual work. When I got the International Sales Director job at Steeles, I expected to be in that job for at least four years so I didn't worry too much about career advancement. Besides, Giselle had her eyes on Tony's position and I didn't need to compete with her as well as getting to grips with the Sales team and the Regional Sales Managers.

However, for your personal advancement through any organization, you need to plan what level you want to achieve in what time scale. This doesn't necessarily mean promotion, it can also mean job advancement in your present position. New Year is always the traditional time of year to do this. You could also use your anniversary date when you started with your present employer. Write down your goals and objectives for the next twelve months and get stuck in. Put them in a drawer somewhere at the back and come back to them when you review your progress and plan your next set of goals.

Giselle told me she planned to have Tony's job within five years. That gave her five planning periods to achieve her objectives, which as we all know turned out so disastrously for her. We could use the three P's here... if we wanted to be cruel...

Piss Poor Planning Giselle!

You will also need to plan on how to best do your existing job. This is not hard as you basically just do it. However, I'd recommend short term goals of three months duration to help with your planning. I know I personally needed to have visited all of my major customers within the first three months of starting my job at Steeles. Once that had been achieved I was able to better plan where to put more sales effort for the maximum benefit of the company. You have a similar opportunity in your present position, good astute short term planning will help you achieve your long term goals. Make sure they dovetail into each other and just do it!

Remember to organize yourself to achieve the best result with the least effort. That doesn't mean shirking, as we already know there is no substitute for hard work, but good planning and organization will enable you to enjoy the job without it killing you. Bella are you listening?

If you're higher up in the organization and have staff working under you then learn to delegate! I always thought, even in the early days, that Des Martin would be a good employee to delegate some of my lesser important jobs to. He's intelligent, very capable, and it was fun for me to train up his man management skills. Now look where he is in the organization... Managing Director.

Jim Thompson of course was my admin manager and he always dealt with the brunt of my paperwork, but he loved it and it was a wonderful win-win situation as I could get on with the bigger stuff like meeting new clients and developing the existing ones.

We women are better than men at delegating. It's a prime female skill so don't get put off by the jargon and serious sounding stuff.
You can do it, just plan!

Chapter 5

Self-Belief;

Self-belief is an area some women can find hard to relate to, but you have no reasons to. Believing in yourself is very important, let's put it this way, if you don't why should anyone else? When I had my job interview at Steele's they put me through a very tough interview process by anyone's standards. If I had no or little self-belief in myself, I would have cracked early on and wouldn't have gotten the job of my dreams. The next step in my personal career ladder.

If you have no support at home or from fellow workers then this can make it harder, so again use a mentor, even if it's books or digital stuff. If you're really up against a wall, use me! Bella, and

Giselle in the early days, were both great supporters of mine at work and I knew Tony was there for me as well. It does help that he hired me of course as he didn't want to be associated with failure. So look to the person in the organization who hired you for support, you may be surprised at how helpful they'll be.

Self-belief is less of a problem for men as they are more confident, it's that ego thing again. But believe me it doesn't mean they are better than us! To help build your self-belief complete tasks which help make you believe in yourself. Remember nothing succeeds like success, just think of all your good points and work to them. Don't just sit in a corner and do nothing, you have to make a start as your self-belief will only develop over time. Take baby steps and don't try and rush it. Bella was just a quiet receptionist when I first met her in Tony's office, and now, well, she's in charge of the complete Steeles sales team... doing my old job. Amazing!

Don't get me wrong, Bella's ego hasn't changed, and she doesn't go around the offices saying she's the greatest Sales Director ever, Giselle would sock her one for sure. But she shows a quiet confidence, she believes in herself, and that empowers her to do greater things. You too need to be quietly confident.

It's always hard to learn to cope with criticism but remember if someone is being unreasonable it says more about them than you. As I keep saying, Sir James tends to lead with his mouth, but as he's the Chairman, I suppose it's his right. If you find it hard to take criticism, then work it through by doing exercise. Walk, cycle, go to the gym and get the adrenaline out of your system. This really works! I had to take a decent break when I got terminated... but that's another story.

One tip which I have found very useful in defusing difficult situations is to apologize even when it's not your fault. I used this technique in a very obtuse way when I found myself in the maze with Jim Stirling. This was his pre-operation days and I pretended to myself that it was my fault that he wasn't getting enough friction to enable his satisfaction. I worked on trying to give him a better experience even though it was not my fault, and got the business. Result!

When building your self-belief try to control your inner chatterbox if it's telling you,

What if I fail;
I can't do that;
Instead think, 'Yes I can!!'
Be positive at all times, a good mental attitude will work wonders and get you to the top of the corporate tree. That's why I'm where I am today, number one in a multi-billion Euro company. If I can do it, then you can do it!

Chapter 6

Attention to detail;

This is where we women excel, it's an essential skill in business but often overlooked. Women are good at attention to detail but don't fall into the trap of being too obsessive. Good enough is good enough, especially if you're working to a strict time schedule. Remember, it doesn't have to be perfect and if you think it should be then you'll never achieve it anyway.

Steeles development team at the pots and pans factory had big problems when they were perfecting the Tri Oxy Brillo range. But people accepted the initial teething problems as the range was cutting edge in the kitchen utensil market. Indeed, that brand has changed the world when it comes to cookware. Their attention to detail pulled them through and it's important to note that often you can only learn by doing.

Attention to detail is applicable to everything we do. If you get something wrong people will soon tell you about the problems.
If they all say the same thing then it needs fixing, if it's lots of different comments then they're less important. Of course, you should check them out, but don't spend valuable time rectifying something which is irrelevant to the whole project.

What goes wrong is always what you least expect. This is the theory of unknown unknowns discussed mostly in military circles. I never expected Peter Rouse to start writing sex symbols in mud on my naked body in the maze.

Would you? I learnt that day that you can't control everything but you can certainly control your reactions to any situation.

There is one warning I think you need to consider when paying attention to detail and that is, the more you focus on details the more you can lose the big picture. Try to avoid this pitfall by always taking an overview of your work. Think as though you are the customer or the person who will receive your piece of work or end product. This could be anything from an internal report to a sales pitch but by considering the recipients needs you can't go wrong. This is one thing I'm trying to teach my current Directors in Germany, but as they're all male, it's proving a bit of a battle. One of course I'll win! After all I'm the CEO!!

Chapter 7;

Coping with stress;

Many people think this is just an office related problem, but you can see it everywhere in life. Perhaps in the competitive world of business and commerce it's more obvious. It can make you short tempered and disagreeable and one of the best ways to deal with it is to make an effort to be pleasant and treat others as you would like to be treated. Giselle really needed to follow this bit of advice.

The best way to achieve this level of tolerance is to relax in the evenings if only for an hour or so and certainly one day a week. Our American guru Stephen Covey calls it 'sharpening the saw.'

Find a way to relax such as the gym, doing a bit of cooking, a weekend break, going out for dinner with friends or just staying in bed for that few hours longer at the weekend. That works best for me and if you can combine a bit of business with pleasure, then you have the perfect scenario. I know Peter and Cristina Rouse agree with me and that's great as they are my mentors. But I do have to make the time to share in their company and lessen my stress levels.

It really doesn't matter how you do it but you must chill out sometime or you'll become stressed. You need to make time to do this or you will get ill. I used to worry about Giselle when she became married to Tony, I thought they never relaxed, it was all business, business, business. She even talked business when we were chilling at the

Pentra on Friday afternoons. Then, when she betrayed the company and Tony, as we later found out, her stress levels must have been through the roof. She certainly was a "Special One".

If you have children try to make time to do something with them.
Eat a special meal together, go to the park, have a weekend away with them and most importantly protect your holidays. You don't get those years back so make use of them. Your kids will thank you for it in later years as I did my Mum and Dad for taking me on all those summer trips to the wine chateaux of France.

Avoid negative people as they'll bring you down and in doing so increase your stress levels. It's hard to be totally positive if someone is continually criticizing you, what you do or how you're doing it. Who you mix with both socially and at work determines your future so think about, how and with whom, you spend your time. Keep your stress levels low and you'll succeed and move up the corporate ladder... just as I did!

Chapter 8

Learn from your mistakes;

We all make them and the professionals amongst us accept this and then learn from them. The person who never made a mistake never learnt anything and similarly the person who cannot take criticism can never improve. Admit to your mistakes as covering them up only works in a large organization... and even then only for a short time and never in small companies like Steele's.

It never ceased to amaze me how much information the secretarial staff gleaned about Steeles over the course of a week. That of course was the information Bella and Giselle told me about when we were the original Glee

Team... happy days. Goodness alone knows what they didn't tell me. It's also one of the reasons Cristina Rouse works out of the reception desk. She'll get to hear about all the mistakes being made throughout the company and be able to take action quickly... unless they're hers of course!

Women have great skills in this area as we are not so ego driven as men. I keep mentioning ego as it's very important you don't allow it to affect your decisions. If you make a mistake, admit and rectify it. Even the best people make mistakes, the mighty Walt Disney Company got lost in the 1980s but it's a winner today.

Just make sure you learn from your experience and change your strategy. This is vital to your future success.

Remember, there is no such word as can't, the only failure is not to learn.

Chapter 9;

Leadership;

In time, like me, you will find your job will put you in charge of other employees. Here you become the captain and you'll take the helm of your department. It's a very exciting time for you, but perhaps one of trepidation for your staff. It will also be lonely especially if there are no other colleagues with your levels of responsibility. At Steele's I was pretty much the only person at my level. Tony was my boss and I answered to him, no one else. That made me the leader of my team. The RSM's were the bulk of my responsibilities and I think it's fair to say they were reasonably concerned for their jobs when I was appointed.

Tony took a fair amount of criticism higher up the company when he told me he didn't need wholesale sackings of the sales force. It was my job to assess the sales operation and make my own decisions. That was good leadership, there was no sense in him doing my job. As you know, the sales team survived intact and indeed generated some strong sales performances. This again was what leadership is about, getting your staff to perform at a high but sustainable level.

If you're new to leadership then you'll have to grow into the job and take 100% responsibility. Remember you are now the boss. Never blame others for mistakes you or your staff make.

Likewise, always give credit where credit is due. I hate it when superiors take all the praise for a job well done leaving their staff unrewarded.

Decision making is another important characteristic of good leadership skills. Never shirk your responsibility, assess the situation and make the informed decision. The RSM's at Steeles knew exactly where I stood on developing the business. If they needed a bit of extra discount to clinch a deal, they didn't wring their hands and worry about asking me about it, they told me and we make the decision. They felt empowered because they'd been included, it's a wonderful win-win!

Setting a good example is also very important in leadership. Staff will be much more motivated when they see the boss getting involved. This is a part of the job I still adore. Making contact with the customer and developing their business with my organization is one of my biggest pleasures. You may think some of my activities are a bit unorthodox, but Tony did outline the finer details of my job at my interview. He left nothing to chance again showing his excellent leadership qualities. It's a shame he can't pick his lovers with equal success.

Leadership has many facets, always try and learn from an experienced member of the company... usually the person who hired you in the first place and if you have an outside mentor all the better.

Chapter 10;

Mentors;

Throughout this book I've been mentioning the word mentor time and time again. I make no apology for it as it's a very important concept to understand and to use. A mentor is someone with skills to help you learn and develop your expertise. Sadly, they are very difficult to come across and very often they cannot be real people unless you are very lucky. Tony my old boss was a good mentor for me but that's all gone now with my new role as his major competitor. However, if you can find someone who's not involved with your work, then that is an ideal situation. For me that is still Peter and Cristina Rouse, though if I'm in the USA, Jim Stirling's door is always open.

Perhaps we'll merge the companies some day?

If you can't find a physical mentor you can use books or digital stuff, YouTube clips, podcasts and so on.
(Why not this one?)
There is no stigma in using these resources, just pick one mentor initially and follow their thoughts and how they relate to your situation. As you develop you will want to bring in more mentors, this is fine, just don't run before you can walk. One good mentor is better than five mediocre ones.

Here are some Rocky, Wilma and I have used;
Robert Kiyosaki;
Stephen Covey;

Remember the people you associate with the most in your daily life will influence you more than you think. Ask yourself what do they do for a living? Are they in a business orientated career? Perhaps they are medics, lawyers, dentists or accountants? Try to find some contacts who are doing what you do in business. Find a group on social media such as Facebook and take it from there. If there isn't one, create one!

Here is a wide ranging list of possible mentors for you to read up. Sadly there's only one woman... apart from myself, but together we can change this! I feel that the gender of the writer isn't important as it's their message that is and you can often find articles by and for women in magazines. Try to read widely and remember you are never too old to learn.

Stephen Covey; Seven Habits of Highly Effective People Series;

Max Gunther; The Zurich Axioms;

Robert Kiyosaki; Rich Dad Series;

Richard Branson; Business Stripped Bare;
one of my all-time favorites!

Jim Rogers; Adventure Capitalist Series;

Stephen D Levitt and Stephen J Dubner, Freakanomics Series;

Joe Cole and Vicki Dominguez; Your Money or Your Life;

Thomas J Stanley and William D Danko; The Millionaire Next Door;

George S Clesson; The Richest Man in Babylon;

Napoleon Hill, Think and Grow Rich;

Niall Ferguson; The Ascent of Money;

Seth Godin; The Purple Cow Series;

William Rees Mogg and James Dale Davidson; The Sovereign Individual;

Belinda Blumenthal & Rocky Flintstone; Belinda's Business Tips for Go Getters;

Conclusion;

This book is all about people and especially women in business. This is what I am as Belinda Blumenthal, this is what I do. I've been quoted as saying, 'When you get what you want, you feel great.'

This is what I want you to achieve. The ten tips which Rocky and I've outlined are all capable of making you a better business woman, a better business person.

The most important tools which anyone needs, to be successful are;
Develop good communication skills;
Know your strengths and what your unique selling point is;
Be a good networker;
Be very hard working;

If you have all these then you are ahead of the ball game. Being able to understand technology and the use of it is a bonus, this is something which can be learnt. The ability to plan ahead successfully, having self-belief in yourself and good attention to detail skills will stand you in good stead all your business career.

The ability to cope with stress and to learn from your mistakes is something you will learn on the job. This is an area where you can learn from a mentor, it is so important to try and develop this sector of your business skills. In time you will become a leader and having a good mentor will greatly assist you in your early days. Try to treat others as you would like to be treated yourself. Never be afraid to become a Mentor to someone else!

Above all Carpe Diem; Seize the day!